# ECHOES OF MARGINALIZATION

## Unveiling Social Discrimination in Arundhati Roy's The God of Small Things

**Author**

**Dr. Prabha Parmar**
Associate Professor
Department of English
FOAHSS, Motherhood University
Roorkee, Uttarakhand


**Co-author**

**Shahjadi Ansari**
B.A, M.A (English) Gold Medalist

First Published in 2024
By
**Notion Press Media Pvt. Ltd,**
7, Red Cross Road
Egmore, Chennai, Tamilnadu, 600008
Email Id: publish@notionpress.com



For permission requests, write to the author
Dr. Prabha Parmar, Author
Email id- prabhaparmar12@gmail.com

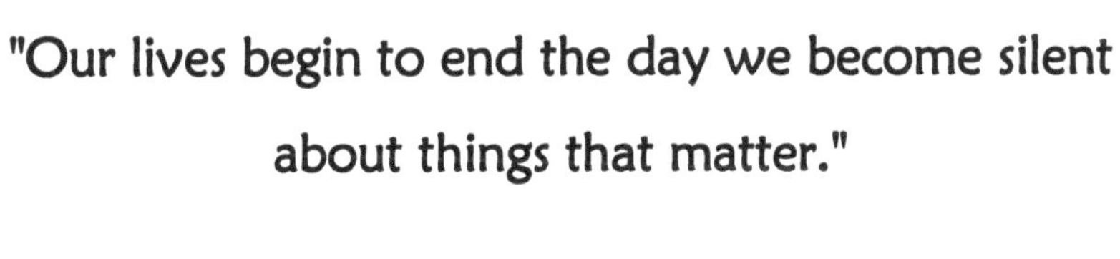

"Our lives begin to end the day we become silent
about things that matter."


- Martin Luther King Jr.

# Content

# Preface

*Echoes of Marginalization: Unveiling Social Discrimination in Arundhati Roy's The God of Small Things* delves into the intricate and poignant portrayal of social discrimination in one of contemporary literature's most celebrated works. Arundhati Roy's debut novel, awarded the Booker Prize in 1997, is not just a narrative of personal tragedy and familial bonds but also a profound commentary on the entrenched systems of caste and social hierarchy in Indian society.

This book seeks to explore the multifaceted dimensions of marginalization that Roy meticulously weaves into her story. *The God of Small Things* is set in the lush, verdant landscape of Kerala, yet beneath its picturesque exterior lies a brutal reality of systemic oppression and social exclusion. Through the lives of its characters—Ammu, Velutha, Estha, and Rahel—Roy exposes the devastating impact of rigid social stratification on individual lives and relationships.

In examining this novel, *Echoes of Marginalization* will guide readers through the historical and cultural contexts that inform the social dynamics depicted in the story. By analyzing key themes such as the caste system, gender inequality, and the repercussions of colonialism, this book aims to provide a deeper understanding of the social fabric that shapes the characters' destinies.

Arundhati Roy's narrative technique, her non-linear storytelling, rich symbolism, and vivid imagery, serves as a powerful tool to highlight the pervasive nature of discrimination. This preface sets the stage for a detailed exploration of these literary devices and how they contribute to the overarching theme of social injustice.

Throughout this book, we will dissect the pivotal moments and relationships that define *The God of Small Things*, revealing how Roy's portrayal of love, loss, and defiance resonates with broader social and political issues. We will also consider the critical reception of the novel and its place within the larger canon of postcolonial literature.

It is our hope that *Echoes of Marginalization* will not only enrich your appreciation of Arundhati Roy's masterful storytelling but also inspire a greater awareness of the ongoing struggles against social discrimination. By shining a light on the small things, the seemingly inconsequential details that cumulatively shape lives, this book underscores the importance of recognizing and challenging the systemic forces that perpetuate inequality.

Thank you for embarking on this journey. Together, let us uncover the echoes of marginalization that reverberate through the pages of *The God of Small Things*, and in doing so, contribute to the broader discourse on social justice and human dignity.


Sincerely,
Author & Co-author

# Acknowledgement

Writing *Echoes of Marginalization: Unveiling Social Discrimination in Arundhati Roy's The God of Small Things* has been a journey of intellectual and emotional exploration, one that would not have been possible without the support and encouragement of many individuals.

First and foremost, I would like to express my deepest gratitude to Arundhati Roy, whose remarkable work has been both an inspiration and a guiding light throughout this project. Her fearless examination of social issues and her powerful storytelling have provided a rich foundation for this analysis.

To my research assistant and also the co-author of this book, Shahjadi Ansari, thank you for your diligent efforts in gathering and organizing the vast array of resources that have informed this work. Your contributions have been essential in bringing this book to fruition.

A special thanks goes to my parents, whose love and support have sustained me throughout this endeavor. To my husband, Dr. Ajay Singh Parmar, your patience, understanding, and unwavering belief in me have been a source of strength.

I would also like to acknowledge the contributions of the editorial team at Notion Press. Your meticulous attention to detail and commitment to excellence have greatly enhanced the quality of this book. Thank you for believing in this project and for your unwavering support.

Finally, I am deeply appreciative of the readers who engage with this work. It is my hope that *Echoes of Marginalization* will inspire a deeper understanding of the social issues explored in *The God of Small Things* and contribute to the ongoing conversation about social justice and equality.

Thank you all for your support and encouragement.


Sincerely,
Dr. Prabha Parmar

Arundhati Roy was an Indian woman author who mostly concentrated on psychological concerns in the lives of female characters who were subjected to emotional pain in patriarchal societies. She successfully projected the damaged thoughts of abused Indian women using their talent. The representation of women characters in her story represented her feminist viewpoint, mindset, and approach. She delved deeply into the psyches of persecuted women characters by preserving their feminine viewpoint and exposing their challenges, which were the result of emotional and psychological abnormalities typical among Indian women. Arundhati Roy is an award-winning Indian author who is highly involved in the country's social issues. She has illustrated all of the challenges that the average person faces. She has attempted to draw our attention to the society's most pressing issues.

Arundhati Roy, born on November 24, 1961, in Shillong, India, is a prolific author, activist, and public intellectual whose work has had a profound impact on contemporary literature and social discourse. Best known for her debut novel, *The God of Small Things*, Roy's literary and activist contributions extend far beyond the realm of fiction. Her writing traverses themes of social justice, political critique, and human rights, establishing her as a formidable voice in both Indian and global contexts.

Roy's early life was marked by a blend of diverse cultural influences. Her mother, Mary Roy, was a prominent social activist and educator, while her father was a tea planter. This unique upbringing in the diverse landscape of India imbued Roy with a deep understanding of the country's complex social fabric. Her education at the Delhi School of Architecture also played a pivotal role in shaping her creative vision and narrative style.

Published in 1997, *The God of Small Things* catapulted Roy to international fame, earning her the prestigious Booker Prize. The novel, set in the lush backwaters of Kerala, explores themes of forbidden love, caste discrimination, and the traumatic impact of historical events on individual lives. Roy's lyrical prose and intricate storytelling captivated readers and critics alike, marking her as a significant literary figure.

The novel's success was not merely due to its compelling narrative but also its deep engagement with the socio-political realities of India. Roy's ability to intertwine personal and political narratives set a new benchmark for Indian English literature, challenging traditional storytelling methods and bringing marginalized voices to the forefront.

Beyond her achievements in fiction, Roy is renowned for her unwavering commitment to social justice and activism. Her essays and non-fiction works, such as *The Algebra of Infinite Justice* and *Field Notes on Democracy*, offer incisive critiques of globalization, neoliberalism, and state-sponsored violence. Roy's activism is characterized by her fearless opposition to oppressive systems, whether they be governmental policies, corporate exploitation, or societal norms.

Roy's activism is not confined to her writing. She has been a vocal advocate on numerous issues, including the Narmada Dam project, India's nuclear policies, and the treatment of indigenous communities. Her outspoken nature has often placed her at odds with powerful entities, but it has also earned her respect and admiration from those who value justice and equity.

Arundhati Roy's literary style is distinguished by its poetic quality, rich imagery, and the seamless blending of the personal with the political. Her narrative voice is both intimate and expansive, capable of delving into the minutiae of human experience while simultaneously addressing broader societal concerns. Themes of love, loss, identity, and resistance recur throughout her work, reflecting her deep empathy for the human condition and her critical perspective on societal structures.

In *The God of Small Things*, for instance, Roy employs a non-linear narrative structure, shifting between past and present to reveal the complexities of her characters' lives. This technique not only enhances the emotional depth of the story but also underscores the enduring impact of historical injustices.

Arundhati Roy's significance as a writer extends beyond her literary achievements. She represents a powerful voice in the global dialogue on human rights, environmental conservation, and social justice. Her works have been translated into multiple languages, reaching a diverse international audience and inspiring countless readers and activists worldwide.

Roy's legacy is multifaceted. As a novelist, she has expanded the horizons of Indian literature, introducing new narrative forms and addressing pressing social issues. As an activist, she has exemplified the role of the writer as a public intellectual, using her platform to advocate for change and challenge the status quo. Her contributions to literature and activism have solidified her place as one of the most influential writers of our time. Her ability to weave together the personal and political, coupled with her relentless pursuit of justice, makes her a unique and vital voice in contemporary discourse. As we explore her works and their impact, we gain not only a deeper appreciation for her literary talent but also an enhanced understanding of the complex world we inhabit. Roy's enduring relevance and powerful storytelling continue to inspire and provoke thought, cementing her legacy as a writer of significant consequence.

Arundhati Roy's family background is as diverse and multifaceted as her literary works. Her mother, is a prominent figure in her own right. An accomplished educator and social activist, Mary Roy is best known for her legal battle against the Syrian Christian inheritance laws in Kerala, which discriminated against women. Her successful challenge led to a landmark Supreme Court ruling in 1986 that granted Syrian Christian women in Kerala equal rights to their ancestral property. This victory not only changed the lives of countless women but also highlighted Mary Roy's determination and resilience, traits that undeniably influenced her daughter.

Mary Roy''s progressive outlook and commitment to social justice played a crucial role in shaping Arundhati's worldview. The intellectual environment provided by her mother, who founded the Pallikoodam School (formerly Corpus Christi) in Kottayam, Kerala, encouraged critical thinking and a strong sense of independence in young Arundhati.

Her father, Rajib Roy, was a Bengali Hindu tea planter from Calcutta (now Kolkata). His work took him to various tea estates in Assam and Meghalaya, exposing Arundhati to the diverse cultural landscapes of India from an early age. Despite his professional background, Rajib Roy's personal life was marked by turmoil. He separated from Mary Roy when Arundhati was just two years old, a separation that led Mary Roy to raise Arundhati and her brother, Lalit, as a single mother.

Following her parents' separation, Arundhati moved with her mother and brother to Kerala, where she spent much of her childhood. Growing up in Aymanam, a village in Kerala, Roy was immersed in the lush, tropical environment that would later provide the setting for her acclaimed novel, *The God of Small Things*. Her experiences in this region deeply influenced her understanding of social hierarchies, local customs, and the intricate relationships within her community.

Despite the challenges of single parenthood, Mary Roy ensured that Arundhati and her brother received a well-rounded education.

This upbringing, characterized by a blend of strict discipline and intellectual freedom, fostered Arundhati's early interest in literature, politics, and social issues.

Her formal education began at the schools her mother founded. She later attended the Lawrence School, Lovedale in the Nilgiri Hills of Tamil Nadu, known for its academic rigor and diverse student body. This experience further broadened her horizons, exposing her to different cultures and ideas.

Roy went on to study architecture at the Delhi School of Architecture. Her time there was not only formative in terms of her professional development but also instrumental in shaping her creative sensibilities. It was during this period that she met her first husband, architect Gerard Da Cunha, though their marriage was short-lived. The discipline of architecture, with its emphasis on design, structure, and form, influenced Roy's approach to writing, evident in the intricate and carefully crafted narratives of her literary works.

The confluence of her parents' diverse backgrounds, her mother's activism, and her own eclectic educational journey played a significant role in shaping Arundhati Roy's perspective and literary voice. Her writing is imbued with a deep sensitivity to social injustices, a nuanced understanding of India's cultural and political complexities, and a poetic appreciation of the natural world.

In *The God of Small Things*, for example, Roy draws heavily from her childhood experiences in Kerala, blending the personal with the political to create a rich, evocative narrative. The novel's exploration of caste discrimination, familial bonds, and forbidden love reflects the various influences that have shaped Roy's life.

Arundhati Roy's journey into writing was a nuanced evolution shaped by her diverse experiences and keen observations of the world around her. From her early career in filmmaking to her debut as a novelist, Roy's transition showcased her distinctive voice and marked the beginning of her influential literary career.

Before achieving international acclaim as a novelist, Arundhati Roy embarked on a career in various creative fields, each contributing uniquely to her eventual success as a writer. Initially drawn to the visual arts, Roy pursued a career in filmmaking during her early adulthood. She worked on several documentary films that explored social and political issues in India. This experience honed her storytelling abilities and deepened her engagement with the socio-political realities of her country.

Roy's involvement in screenwriting and acting provided her with insights into narrative construction and character development. These skills would later prove invaluable in crafting the complex and multi-dimensional characters that populate her fiction.

Alongside her creative pursuits, Roy emerged as a prominent voice in activism and journalism. Her essays and articles, often published in major Indian and international publications, garnered attention for their incisive critiques of social injustice, economic inequality, and environmental degradation. This period marked the beginning of her transition from visual storytelling to the written word.

Arundhati Roy's literary debut, *The God of Small Things*, published in 1997, catapulted her to literary stardom and earned her the prestigious Booker Prize. The novel, set in the southern Indian state of Kerala, intricately weaves together themes of forbidden love, caste discrimination, and familial bonds against the backdrop of a changing social landscape.

*The God of Small Things* is renowned for its lyrical prose, non-linear narrative structure, and evocative depiction of Kerala's cultural milieu. Roy's exploration of social hierarchies and the traumatic consequences of societal norms on individual lives resonated deeply with readers and critics alike.

The novel's critical and commercial success established Arundhati Roy as a significant voice in Indian and global literature. It was praised for its narrative complexity, poignant portrayal of characters, and its ability to confront uncomfortable truths about Indian society.

This novel was not only cemented Roy's literary reputation but also set a high standard for Indian English literature. Its exploration of marginalized voices and its critique of power dynamics continue to inspire readers and writers worldwide. The novel remains a landmark work that deftly combines personal storytelling with broader socio-political commentary.

In addition to her fiction, Arundhati Roy's early essays and non-fiction works established her as a fearless critic and advocate for social justice. Her collection of essays, *The Algebra of Infinite Justice*, published in 2002, examines issues such as globalization, corporate power, and the impact of neoliberal economic policies on marginalized communities.

Roy's non-fiction writing reflects her deep engagement with pressing social and political issues in India and beyond. She uses her platform to amplify the voices of the marginalized, challenge dominant narratives, and demand accountability from governments and corporations.

Known for her sharp intellect and eloquent prose, Roy's essays blend personal reflection with rigorous analysis. They provoke thought, spark debate, and inspire activism among her readers and supporters. Her transition to writing was marked by a convergence of artistic exploration, social activism, and a deep commitment to storytelling. From her early career in filmmaking and activism to the literary acclaim of *The God of Small Things* and her influential essays, Roy's journey underscores the power of narrative to illuminate social injustices and provoke meaningful change. Her ability to merge personal experience with broader socio-political critique has established her as a formidable voice in contemporary literature and a steadfast advocate for justice and equality.

*The God of Small Things* is a poignant and intricately woven narrative set in the lush, evocative backdrop of Kerala, India. It explores themes of love, loss, betrayal, and the rigid social hierarchies that pervade Indian society. The story unfolds through the eyes of two twins, Rahel and Estha, whose lives are forever altered by a series of tragic events and personal choices.

The novel is primarily set in the village of Aymanam, situated amidst Kerala's backwaters. The richly detailed setting serves not only as a geographical backdrop but also as a metaphorical space where social, political, and personal histories converge.

At the heart of the novel are Rahel and Estha, whose childhood innocence is shattered by family secrets, societal expectations, and the harsh realities of caste discrimination. Other central characters include their mother Ammu, their grandaunt Baby Kochamma, and Velutha, a talented Untouchable (or Dalit) carpenter who becomes entangled in a forbidden love affair.

Roy employs a non-linear narrative structure, shifting fluidly between past and present, weaving together memories, dreams, and reflections. This fragmented storytelling technique enhances the novel's emotional depth and underscores the interconnectedness of personal and historical narratives.

The novel explores various forms of love – romantic, familial, and platonic – and the betrayal that often accompanies these relationships. Roy confronts the deeply entrenched caste system in India, highlighting the oppressive structures that marginalize and dehumanize individuals based on their caste identities.

The characters in the novel grapple with profound losses – of innocence, of loved ones, and of the possibility of a better future. Trauma, both personal and collective, permeates their lives and shapes their identities.

Against the backdrop of India's political upheavals in the 1960s and 1970s, Roy critiques the societal norms and political forces that perpetuate inequality and division. Arundhati Roy's prose is celebrated for its lyrical beauty, vivid imagery, and poetic language. Her writing captures the sensory richness of Kerala's landscapes while delving into the complexities of human emotions and relationships.

This novel remains a seminal work in contemporary literature, praised for its narrative innovation, thematic depth, and social critique. It challenges readers to confront uncomfortable truths about power, privilege, and the enduring legacy of colonialism in post-independence India.

This is more than a novel; it is a literary masterpiece that continues to resonate with readers worldwide. Through its compelling characters, evocative setting, and profound exploration of social issues, Roy crafts a narrative that is both deeply personal and universally relevant. Her ability to merge the intimate details of individual lives with broader socio-political commentary underscores her status as a visionary storyteller and a fearless advocate for justice and equality.

Her impact on Indian literature and the global literary scene is profound and multifaceted, extending beyond her acclaimed novels to her fearless advocacy for social justice and environmental causes.

Through her writing, Roy confronts and critiques deeply entrenched cultural norms, such as caste discrimination, gender inequality, and the legacy of colonialism. Her work encourages readers to confront uncomfortable truths about Indian society and its complexities. Roy gives voice to marginalized communities, highlighting their struggles and resilience amidst social and economic injustices. Her characters reflect the diversity and complexity of Indian society, contributing to a more inclusive literary landscape.

Roy's novels have been translated into numerous languages and have garnered international acclaim, making her a prominent figure in global literature. Her ability to weave together personal stories with universal themes resonates with readers worldwide.

Beyond fiction, her essays and non-fiction works are powerful critiques of globalization, neoliberalism, and environmental degradation. She uses her platform to advocate for human rights, environmental sustainability, and economic justice.

Her role as a public intellectual and activist amplifies her impact beyond literature. She fearlessly speaks truth to power, challenging governments, corporations, and societal norms that perpetuate inequality and injustice.

Roy's advocacy extends to environmental causes, particularly against large-scale development projects that threaten indigenous communities and ecosystems. Her activism reflects a deep commitment to ecological sustainability and the rights of marginalized communities. Through her writing and activism, she inspires individuals and movements to engage critically with issues of social, economic, and environmental justice. Her work encourages collective action and solidarity in the pursuit of a more just and equitable world.

Her contributions to literature and social causes have left an indelible mark on contemporary discourse. Her writing continues to provoke thought, inspire empathy, and challenge readers to reconsider their perspectives on power, privilege, and the human condition.

Arundhati Roy's impact on Indian literature and the global literary scene is characterized by her bold storytelling, incisive social critique, and unwavering commitment to justice. Her work transcends the boundaries of fiction to address pressing socio-political issues, leaving a lasting legacy that resonates with readers and activists alike. As a writer and activist, Roy exemplifies the transformative power of literature to provoke change and advocate for a more inclusive and compassionate world.

In *The God of Small Things*, Roy crafts a narrative that delves deeply into the heart of India's entrenched social hierarchies, with the caste system as one of its most pervasive and insidious elements. This chapter examines how Roy portrays the caste system and its impact on the lives of her characters, revealing the multifaceted nature of caste-based discrimination and its far-reaching consequences.

To fully grasp the implications of the caste system within the novel, it is essential to understand its historical and cultural roots. Originating from ancient Hindu scriptures, the caste system stratifies society into rigid hierarchical groups, with each caste assigned specific roles and duties. Despite legal measures aimed at abolishing caste discrimination, these deeply ingrained social divisions continue to influence contemporary Indian society, often dictating one's social status, occupation, and personal relationships. At the center of Roy's exploration of caste is Velutha, a Paravan or "Untouchable," whose life and fate poignantly illustrate the brutal realities of caste oppression. Velutha's skill and integrity as a carpenter contrast sharply with the societal prejudice that seeks to diminish his humanity. His illicit relationship with Ammu, an upper-caste woman, serves as a powerful narrative device to expose the violent repercussions of transgressing caste boundaries.

Velutha's tragic end underscores the dehumanizing effects of the caste system and the lengths to which society will go to maintain its rigid hierarchies.

The Ipe family, central to the narrative, embodies the complexities of caste dynamics within a relatively privileged context. While they are not part of the highest caste, their social standing still affords them a degree of power and influence. Characters like Baby Kochamma and Mammachi display an internalized adherence to caste norms, reinforcing these oppressive structures even as they navigate their own struggles within the patriarchal society. The family's interactions with Velutha, marked by both reliance on his labor and disdain for his social position, highlight the pervasive nature of caste prejudices.

Roy's depiction of caste goes beyond individual interactions to reflect the broader social stratification in Kerala. The novel's setting in Ayemenem, with its lush landscapes and tightly-knit community, serves as a microcosm of Indian society, where caste dictates social interactions and relationships. The story vividly illustrates how caste-based discrimination is woven into the fabric of daily life, affecting everything from employment opportunities to personal freedoms.

Roy employs rich symbolism and innovative narrative techniques to emphasize the impact of the caste system. The non-linear storytelling, with its interwoven timelines and perspectives, mirrors the fragmented lives of the characters, fractured by the oppressive forces of caste. Symbols such as the History House and the river reflect the societal boundaries and the ever-present, inescapable nature of caste discrimination.

By unraveling the intricacies of the caste system, *The God of Small Things* calls attention to the urgent need for social change. Roy's narrative not only exposes the cruelty and injustice perpetuated by caste hierarchies but also challenges readers to confront these realities and consider their implications in the contemporary world. Through this exploration, the novel becomes a powerful vehicle for advocating equality and human dignity, urging a reexamination of deeply held societal norms.

In this chapter, we will delve deeper into these themes, analyzing how Roy's portrayal of the caste system in *The God of Small Things* serves as both a critique of historical injustices and a poignant commentary on their persistent presence in modern society. By examining the experiences of Velutha, the Ipe family, and the broader social context, we aim to uncover the layers of meaning that make this novel a profound exploration of caste and its devastating effects.

In The God of Small Things, history is the source of all misery, agony, and chaos. Velutha and Ammu are the victims of India's social past, which includes centuries of abhorrent rituals and injustice. From the distant past to the present, Indian society has experienced shameful customs and the ills of caste and gender inequality. Velutha and Ammu are victims of Indian society's brutal atrocities and inflexible norms. The main caste structure shapes society in *The God of Small Things*. Characters are divided into caste groups, each of which may discriminate against one another. The Indian caste system is divided into five groups: Brahmins (priests), Kshatriyas (warriors), Vaishyas (merchants, landowners), Shudras (servants), and Untouchables (slaves) (cobblers, street sweepers, latrine cleaners). The caste of an individual is decided from birth depending on their family's caste. Religious divides are depicted in the narrative through arguments between Mulligan (a Roman Catholic) and Revealed Ipe (a Mathoma), as well as Baby Kochamma's conversion to Catholicism and subsequent lack of suitors. Colonial control brought about socio-political developments that resulted in higher caste Hindus outshining Syrian Christians. *The God of Small Things* is referring to the "untouchable" school founded by the twins' great-grandfather, Estha and Rahel. Despite the fact that many paravans and other low caste people converted to Christianity, they were forced to attend separate churches and therefore remained "untouchables," as Roy points out.They were denied government perks provided for "untouchables" after independence since they were legally Christians and there for casteless. In her novel *The God of Small Things*, Arundhati Roy, a famed Indian English writer, depicts the term untouchability, giving a true image of the untouchable, lower caste people. As a result, this research report is an attempt to comprehend the issues of social discrimination in Arundhati Roy's *The God Of Small Things*. Another significant gender issue was the confirmation of the male-dominated family structure by patriarchal faiths.

The story depicts women's continual battle against the exploitation, pain, and struggle that they face as a result of the male-dominated traditional culture. It discusses the absurdity and unfairness of women's household and social lives. Roy mostly covers issues that affect everyone. Individuals strive for the courage to live as well as the ability to love and be loved. Ammu, for example, is a character. Characters like Velutha or even Rahel and Estha have no origins. Their alienation is what drives them on. From one catastrophe to the next, various additional individuals get sucked in.They are mostly portrayed as love and identity searchers. Both emotionally and psychically disturbed, Ammu and Velutha are driven maniacally by undefined hunger and furious passion, which leads to their demise. They manage to go through life while being incapable of quiet acquiescence and ungrudging pain. Ammu opposes patriarchal dominance, discrimination based on class and caste in public and pays the price with her life. Roy's characters suffer from a lack of parental affection, a troubled childhood, and shattered houses. They are unsatisfied with their lives and frequently prefer to live outside the mainstream. This estrangement is sometimes expressed through unethical relationships and actions. As a result of their alienation from themselves, they go on a frenetic quest for their identity in the environment through self-discovery and self-identification. The story depicts the sorrows of three generations of women—Mammachi, Ammu, and Rahel—who respond to the circumstances in their own unique ways. The three generations of women have diverse perspectives on life and respond to situations in various ways.

This award-winning work depicts the Hindu society's cross-caste and sub-caste social divisions. Even in this postcolonial day, she is outraged by the brutal treatment meted out to the lower classes. Treating a group of individuals with disdain and treating them differently than others is referred to as social discrimination. Untouchability has a significant role in social prejudice. The caste system in India is divided into four groups: Brahmins, Kshatryas, Vaishyas, and Shudras. Brahmins, Kshatryas, and Vaishyas have all of society's rights and have a superior social status. The Shudras, on the other hand, had to struggle to stay alive. They were struggling to make it through the day. They are the untouchables, and their job include cleaning toilets, sewerage, and so forth. It was a turning point in Indian history. The untouchables Velutha and Ammu perished owing to societal factors in Roy's *The God of Small Things*. The untouchables were not permitted to enter the upper-class homes. They were not permitted to stroll along the street. It was forbidden for them to wear shirts. The untouchables kept their mouths covered with their hands when the upper class spoke; only the dirty breath was kept away from the touchables. They were not permitted to carry umbrellas. They were not permitted to enter the temple. In villages, the untouchables had their own street with their own entrance. They were not permitted to drink from the same well as the rest of the group. They had their own well for drinking water. If the untouchable came into contact with the touchable's possessions, they promptly washed them with water. Mammachi explained all of these rituals to the fraternal twins, Estha and Rahel. Pappachi's pickle plant employed Velutha. VellayaPapan, Velutha's father, was the one who introduced him to the Ipe family. Velutha was a skilled artisan and mechanic. He was extremely gifted at such a young age. The Ipe family was pleased with this. Velutha was accompanied to school by Mammachi. He completed his education and returned to the pickle plant.

In *The God of Small Things*, masculine chauvinism is also present. Roy depicts the wretched fate of untouchables as well as the struggle of a woman seeking satisfaction in a patriarchal culture. Velutha, the deity of tiny things, defies social standards by having an affair with a woman from a higher caste. The terrible death of a untouchable by touchable boots of state police is the ultimate result of this love, an incident that makes a mockery of the concept of God. God no longer has authority over little things, but rather they have ultimate power over God, turning him to "The God of loss" (Roy, 265). The work explores the concept of untouchability on two levels. To begin with, there are those who are socially untouchables, or Parvan, who are never granted fundamental human rights. Second, there are metaphorical untouchables among the upper classes. Velutha is "very clever," a skilled carpenter with an engineer's mind, but he's also "The God of Loss. He left no footprints in sand, no ripples in water, no images in mirrors" (Roy, 265) Chacko, unlike Velutha, can get away with his decadence or, as his mother puts it, his man's wants because he is a touchable. When she remarks, Roy has presented the situation in the right light she is correct "Change is one thing. Acceptance is another" (Roy, 279). The patriarchal society depicted in the novel is a patriarchal society. On the one hand, there are characters like Mammachi, Baby Koachmma, and Kochu Maria the cook who reinforce caste, race, and gender divisions. Ammu and the twins, Rahel and Estha, on the other hand, deliberately and intuitively defy these hierarchies. Ammu, the system's most egregious victim, is the quintessential picture of a disadvantaged daughter in a patriarchal culture. "Perhaps Ammu, Estha and Rahel were the worst transgressors. They all broke the rules. They all crossed into forbidden territory. They all tampered with laws that lay down who should be loved and how. And how much" (Roy, 31). The principal character of the tale, Ammu, has barely a sliver of a place in the family. Women's education is undervalued in traditional patriarchal societies. Pappachi, Ammu's father, dislikes spending money on his daughter, and she is never pushed to find her place in the world. Her only chance of survival is via marriage.

"Ammu finished her schooling the same year that her father retired from the job in Delhi and moved to Aymenem. Pappachi insisted that a college education was unnecessary expense for a girl so Ammu had no choice but to leave Delhi and move with him. There was little for a young girl to do in Aymenem other than to wait for marriage proposal" (Roy, 38). After five days of dating, Ammu accepts the first proposal. Ammu had no option but to accept whatever life had in store for her. Her spouse, however, turns out to be a drinker who is incapable of supporting the family. He attempts to persuade Ammu to 'please the boss,' but she refuses, and the couple divorces. She has to deal with ostracism from her community and family as a divorcee. Her female relatives sympathise with her in certain ways, making her aware of the seriousness of her crime of living apart from her husband. "Within first few months of her return to her parent's home; Ammu quickly learned to recognize and despise the ugly face of sympathy. Old female relations with their incipient beards and several wobbling chins made overnight trips to Ayemenem to commiserate her about her divorce. She fought off the urge to slap them."(Roy, 43) A divorced person has no legal right to seek happiness in life. The only option she has is to live a life in limbo, waiting for death. Any attempt on her side to see life in a different light endangers the status quo. She is at odds with society as a whole since she married outside of her group and is also a divorcee. At SophieMol's funeral, it's clear: "Though Ammu, Estha and Rahel were allowed to attend the funeral, they were made to stand separately, not with the rest of the family. Nobody would look at them" (Roy, 5). This injustice is carried out by a group of people who have been victims of injustice themselves. Mammachi, Ammu's mother, who has had to put up with her husband's abuse, excuses Chako's sexual exploitation of female employees, but she can't stand her daughter's liaison with a Parvan. The system's defender, Baby Kochamma, would go to any length to preserve the so-called family honour. The story depicts the process of identifying and classifying Parvans inside upper-class households — those who defy society's unwritten rules in quest of pleasure. Velutha provides what society and family have denied Ammu, Estha, and Rahel. He is the finest buddy of the children in the daylight, who feel stifled in Ayemenem due to their divorced mother. The outside world is unfriendly, and they can only find true happiness in the limited times they spend with Velutha. Ammu encounters him in the dark near the riverbank, a symbol of the social divide between the two classes. Baby Kochamma arrives as the system's caretaker, having spent her life frozen in the past. Velutha, the Untouchable is assassinated by the state police's Touchable Boots. Ammu is exiled and dies alone at the age of thirty-one "a viable, die-able ages."(Roy, 161) The system has a deadly effect on the twins, who are unable to relate to anybody but each other. Estha's marriage fails, and she is content with just her twin brother Rahel, as though returning to her prenatal world of pure innocence. Velutha provides an escape from Aymenem's deterministic reality. For a little while, he offers the opportunity to live in accordance with one's own self. However, the release is really a ruse. Every attempt at personal satisfaction is viewed by the system as a direct challenge to its established set of values. Velutha was a far greater individual. He was a skilled mechanic and artisan. He graduated from high school at the age of sixteen and went on to become a skilled carpenter. He established what he refers to as a "German design sensibility." Valutha had a specific expertise of fixing machinery such as radios, clocks, and water pumps in addition to his carpentry skills. He was the one who examined the plumbing and electrical equipment of the 'Big Ayemenem House'.Mammachi used to say: "If only he hadn't been a Paravan he might have become an engineer"(Roy, 75).Velutha was a wonderful mother and grandmother to Ammu and her children. Despite his generosity, he dies a horrible, humiliating, and terrible death; he becomes a victim of India's brutal caste system. Even though casteism is illegal under the Indian constitution, certain Velutha are still humiliated and forced to drink pee and consume the dung of cruel, barbaric individuals in upper castes in several parts of India. Ammu is in a similar situation. In Indian history, she has been the victim of centuries of male chauvinism. She was abused by her father, Pappachi, who used to beat her and her mother, Mammachi, with a brass vase when she was a youngster. "Not content with having beaten his wife and daughter, he tore down curtains, kicked furniture and smashed a table lamp"(Roy, 181). While her brother was encouraged to seek further education, her father refused to enable her to do so since, in his opinion, "a college education was an unnecessary expense for a girl"(Roy, 38). In India, male chauvinism has a long history. In Indian tradition, a woman's husband was considered her God, and she was expected to submit to his wishes in all circumstances. In Indian history, the practise of "Sati" was observed, on which a widowed woman was denied the right to life after her husband died, and was thus expected to burn herself in his funeral pyre. The widows had their heads tonsured and were not permitted to use cosmetics or attend ceremonies. Many Indian women have died as a result of the dowry system. Many women are being burned alive because they do not comply with their in-laws' requests. In recent times, female foeticide in India has been the biggest crime and disgrace to the country and its society. Her spouse had also molested her. He was an alcoholic who even went so far as to urge his wife to fulfil the sexual desires of his employer, Mr. Hollick, in order to save his job. When Ammu declined to help me, he became enraged "lunged at her, grabbed her hair, and punched her"(Roy, 420). Chacko, Ammu's brother, would instil masculine chauvinism in her. Chacko remarked on her; "What's yours is mine and what's mine is also mine."(Roy, 57). Baby Kochamma would torment her as well. She once made a remark about Ammu, illustrating the situation and fate of a divorced woman in Indian society. "She subscribe wholeheartedly to the commonly held view that a married daughter had no position in her parent's home. As for a divorced daughter, she had no position at all" (Roy, 45). As a result, Ammu died tragically: "thirty one. Not old. Not young. But a viable die-able age" (Roy, 03) .Velutha and Ammu were both victims of the vile caste system and vicious male chauvinism that has plagued India for centuries. In other words, history is the true perpetrator of Velutha and Ammu's pains and terrible deaths in *The God of Small Things*.

In Ammu's instance, she was divorced from her husband, and their parents treated her cruelly. Ammu saw male-chauvinism in her brother Chacko as well. He was completely controlling Ammu's every move. She was handled differently after her divorce than she had been in the past. Because they were born for inter-caste couples, her fraternal twins were likewise mistreated by her family. Velutha develops a bond with Ammu and her twins. They formed a strong bond. The connection between Ammu and Velutha was declared unlawful. They have a strong bond between them. Their clandestine relationship was discovered by family members. Ammu was confined to his room. Because of her romance with Velutha, Ammu was separated from her children. Mammachi was envisaged as their relationship's apex. She believes that if the untouchable touches her daughter, she would become unclean. Ammu, like Velutha, breaches the laws of society. Ammu violates the Ipe family's responsibility. Velutha was accused of being a kidnapper, murderer, and rapist. He was accused of kidnapping Estha and Rahel, raped Ammu, and murdered Sophie Mol. He was arrested on the orders of Ipe's family because of his unlawful relationship with Ammu. Velutha was violently handled in the police station. Baby Kochamma pushed Estha and Rahel to be the witness against Velutha. Ammu was taken aback when she learned that her children were named as witnesses in the case. She began to despise Estha and Rahel. Ammu had been expelled from the family and had been separated from her children. She didn't even consider their children or a family member, and the family members were enraged by her clandestine relationship with the untouchable. The caste system is only abolished in some parts of modern India. Untouchables were still subject to some regulations in India's rural areas.

The untouchables were isolated from the common people, and they resided in a Separate Street at the far end of the hamlet, too far away from the touchables. They were not allowed to enter upper-class homes, nor were they allowed to touch the touchable or their belongings, as was the case in previous India. They were not permitted to visit the temple. The untouchables were permitted to labour in upper-class homes, but they were not invited to family functions. Similarly, the untouchable invited the touchable to a family celebration, but the upper class folks did not show up. History does not alter with the passage of time. The untouchables were granted various rights and privileges by the contemporary Indian government. They were given first priority when it came to employment Velutha was severely abused and suffered major injuries over his body. Ammu went to the police station and told them the truth. She said that Velutha was falsely accused of taking revenge on him by the Ipe family due of their illegal connection. Velutha was discovered to be a communist by the inspector. At long last, the truth was disclosed. Velutha, however, died in the police station as a result of his serious injuries offers and educational scholarships. This resulted in a shift in the caste structure. After all of this, Ammu decides to separate the twins. Their family members did not treat Ammu well. She has been living alone for a number of years, with no one to look after her. Ammu died at the age of 31.

It was not a matter of being young or old, but of being old enough to live. Ammu and Velutha have become prey for society as a result of these social divisions. In *the God of Small Things*, untouchability is a major theme. When Mammachi is talking about the past, he says that the Untouchables were not permitted to walk on public roadways and that they had to wipe their footsteps clean so that no one from a higher caste may step into them by accident. They had to talk with their lips covered so that no one had to breathe in their toxic air. They were not given permission to exist in the first place. This nonexistence is mentioned multiple times throughout the narrative, such as when Velutha leaves no imprints or ripples in the water. As a result, he appears nearly otherworldly and unearthly. The tragedy of the Koachammans is set in this social, political, and religious backdrop. They are too sensitive of their family's status since they are shunned by upper-class Hindus. Roy works with tragedy's traditional elements in a contemporary setting. This family is made up of introverts. Baby Kochamma, Ammu, Chacko, and Pappachi can't seem to get over their issues. They fight the outside world, and their loss leaves them befuddled and frustrated. The feeling of failure manifests itself in the dehumanisation of others around them. The author's implicit claim is that Indian women can withstand a great deal of pain, even torture, but refuse to submit to immorality against their will. Here's an example: "Ammu watches her husband's mouth more as it formed words. She said nothing. He grew uncomfortable and then infuriated by her silence. Suddenly he lunged at her, grabbed her hair, punched her and then passed out from the efforts. Ammu took down the heaviest book she could find in the bookshelf. The Reader's Digest World Atlas and hits him with it as hard as she could. On his head, on his eyes, his back, and shoulders. When he regained consciousness, he was puzzled by his bruises. He apologized abjectly for the violence, but immediately began to badger her about helping with his transfer. This fell into a pattern. Drunken violence followed by post drunken badgering"(Roy, 42). *The God of Small Things* is a scathing attack on Kerala's touchable society's patriarchal mentality, which includes high caste Syrian Christians and high caste Hindus. The geo-cultural truth of Ayemenem is at the foundation of the dilemma of patriarchal superiority and female subordination. Velutha and Vellya, his father, were subjected to some of the most heinous abuse imaginable at the hands of another human being. Untouchables were not allowed to stroll on public roadways, wear clothing that covered their upper bodies, or carry umbrellas during Mammachi's time. When they spoke, they had to cover their lips with their hands to keep their dirty breath away from the people they were speaking to. According to Karl Marx, society has progressed through four epochs: primitive communism, ancient society, feudal society, and capitalist society.

According to Marx, only the first era, known as primitive communism, is devoid of any social stratification based on class. Marx says that persons in this group have more food resources than they require and thus become a member of a more dynamic society. He is the only one who, based on his analysis, distinguishes between the classes. Only money and economic foundations, according to Marx, are the basis of society. He also feels that because his economic underpinnings are strong, it is wealth ownership that gives an individual authority. The dominant class in society is the one that controls the means of food and commodities production. On the other hand, Marx believes that there is a perpetual fight and conflict between the classes, which results in societal changes. However, the competition between the classes leads to one class dominating the other. In this sense, the study's main goal is to highlight the class struggles depicted by Roy in her work, as well as the rudimentary caste system that exists in Indian culture. The Marxist theory's basic foundations are that economics is the foundation of society. It establishes a superstructure in an existing society, with the most economically powerful individual most suited to become a member of the superstructure. It is thought that a high yield is preferable than gaining a large number of production relations. On the other side,

Marxism holds that with the eradication of capitalist owners, the proletariat will rule.Velutha, on the other hand, is a Marxist supporter. But, because Indian Marxism is not above caste restrictions, even the Marxism he believes in is of little service to him in his life and love. Even Ammu's religion, which is based on lofty spiritual concepts, is opposed to her cause. As a result, Roy rightly compares Marxism to Christianity, explaining how both ideologies failed to achieve their lofty goals of changing caste hierarchies and living circumstances. If Marxism is a political theory, Christianity is a spiritual ideology; both seek to uplift the poor and rid the world of injustice and cruelty.However, neither can do much to improve the lives of the poor since attempting to destabilise the present system, no matter how unfair it is, will result in their losing their power base. As a result, both are failures:-

Marxism was a simple substitute for Christianity. Replace God with Marx, Satan with the Bourgeoisie. Heaven with a classless society, the Church with Party, and the form and purpose of the journey remained similar Communism crept into Kerala insidiously. As a reformist movementthat never overtly questioned the traditional values of a caste-ridden, extremely traditionalcommunity. "The Marxists worked from within the communal divides, never challenging them, neverappearing not to". (Roy, 66)

The story depicts Comrade Pillai's hostility to Velutha as a result of Kerala's still severe caste equations. Though he agrees to Chacko that Velutha is an excellent Partyworker, he, like the other party workers, cannot accept Velutha's low caste roots. Many people are disturbed by Velutha's presence because they cannot stand his behaving above his place. This is something his own father points out:"Perhaps it was just a lack ofhesitation. An unwarranted assurance. In the way he walked. The way he held his head.The quiet way he offered suggestions without being asked. Or the quiet way in which hedisregarded suggestions without appearing to rebel". (Roy, 76)They are enraged at Velutha's success in Chacko's workplace simply because he is a paravan – an invincible. As a result, Pillai encourages Chacko to deport him.

"Any benefits that you give (Velutha), naturally others (Upper Caste party workers, who also work inChacko's factory) are resenting it. They see it as a partiality. After all, whatever job he does,carpenter or electrician or whateveritis, for them he is just a Paravan. It is a conditioning they have from birth. This, I myself have told them is wrong. But, frankly speaking, Comrade, Change is onething. Acceptance is another". (Roy, 278)

The claims of Marxism to bring about revolutionary transformations in society are rendered absurd by caste equations, which demolish Marx's philosophy. As Pillai points out, there is always a gap between change and acceptance. Because of this chasm, Ammuand Velutha's love collapses, and with it, their identity fails to flourish and burgeon in the desired way. The failure to provide Ammu and Velutha with a solid identity is therefore a product of the power-alliance between Marxism and Christianity, as well as the socio-religious systems that pre-date both Marxism and Christianity.Unfortunately, History - another important identification marker – is at odds with the characters' identities in the narrative. As the narrative progresses, we learn that the entire Papachi (Ipe) family is trapped in a difficult situation from which escape is neither easy nor conceivable. Because they are all 'anglophiles,' a breed that is anachronistic in today's world, the family is caught outside of history. As Chacko tells the twins "they were all Anglophiles. They were a family ofAnglophiles: Pointed in the wrong direction, trapped outside their own history, andunable to retrace their own steps because their footprints had been swept away". (Roy, 52)

This rootless state of the Ipe family symbolises, in a synecdoche-like fashion, the predicament of all Indians, namely, the loss of memory, personality, and identity. We have lost our tracks and are unable to retrace them due to historical compulsions. As a result, we are not who we say we are, even our aspirations have been doctored, and we have no place in the world. Footprints represent India's historical past in the novel, as well as the loss of historical consciousness.And it is the Indian English writer's obligated duty to retrace and recreate this history's forgotten self.

Roy tries to bring lost pieces of history to light through Rahel's return to Ayemenem and her numerous trips into the past.

What emerges from this process of transcending national barriers is a hybrid entity, the hallmark of the post-national age. The sky-blue Plymouth, the Papachi family's family automobile, is a good metaphor for the postcolonial authors' drive towards hybridity, according to Alex Tickell. Despite the fact that it is an imported car that represents the global, it has been tailored to meet the demands of the local community."On the Plymouth roof-rack, there (is) a four sided, tin-lined plywood billboard that said, on all four sides, in elaborate writing, Paradise Pickles and Preserves. Below the painting there (are) painted bottles of mixed fruit jamand hot-lime pickle in edible oil with labels that said, in elaborate writing, paradise pickels and preserves. And a Kathakali dancer that give the products, says Chacko, "a Regional flavour", which would stan d them in good stead when they enter the Overseas Market" (Roy, 46-47). The novel strongly stresses the relevance of the local in the global economy in this paragraph. The local and the global are not considered as diametrically opposed forces here; rather, they work together to produce truly cosmopolitan environments that incorporate both local and global components.

# GENDER INEQUALITY AND PATRIARCHY

Arundhati Roy depicts the deplorable state of women in society and their inexplicable fight. Three generations of women are born in diverse surroundings in the novel *The God Of Small Things*. Except for the pain of Ammu, the protagonist, Mammachi, and Rahel, the narrative never gives any kind of happiness. Mammachi, Pappachi's wife and a gifted violinist, is an entomologist. She has been in a lot of pain from the beginning of her marriage. He mistreats his wife despite the fact that he is a well-educated man who acts decently. The God of Small Things has a lot of atmosphere, according to my memories of growing up in Kerala. *The God of Small Things* depicts a patriarchal world ruled by men, with societal prejudices and discrimination based on gender, caste, and class. It depicts the divide between the wealthy and the destitute, the affluent and the impoverished, the mighty and the weak, the touchable and the untouchable. The work deftly pierces the layers of nationality, caste, and religion to uncover humanity's basic bones.

The work accurately portrays the status of women in India. It depicts the women's continual battle against the exploitation, torment, and struggle that they face as a result of the male-dominated traditional framework. Ammu and Margaret

Kochamma, the second generation, demonstrate assertiveness and opposition to conventional society's socio-cultural rules. They violate society's moral rules by engaging in sexual freedom. For her intransigence, Ammu pays a high price. In the conservative fictitious village of Ayemenem in Kerala, Ammu is born into a Syrian Catholic Christian family. Ammu's life has been hampered by male chauvinism and gender intolerance. Patriarchy has been a part of her life since she was a youngster. Mammachi and her daughter, Ammu, are subjected to assault by Pappachi, Ammu's father, an emblem of imperial authority. During the cold evenings in Delhi, he has no qualms about beating Ammu and tossing the two out of the house. Ammu's stubborn demeanour tests him. His resentment prevents him from appreciating his wife's effective management of the family's Paradise Pickles plant. Because of his frustration, he finds pleasure in punishing her. Ammu is not allowed to attend school. She marries Baba after five days of meeting to get rid of her patriarchal father. Her situation worsens, though, because her husband is an alcoholic who hits her on a regular basis.She returns to the nightmare of Ayemenem with her twins after her divorce. Because 'die vorce' implies 'dead,' she and her children are humiliated. Both Ammu and Chacko are alienated from each other. Chacko, on the other hand, is warmly welcomed and becomes the property's inheritor. His wastefulness is well-known"Man's Needs"(Roy, 168). Ammu, on the other hand, is considered as a Veshya. She is self-assured and does not ignore her physical requirements. "She wanted her body back" (Roy,

222).She attempts to find fulfilment in her connection with Velutha, but traditional culture forbids a touchable and an untouchable subaltern from being together. Inspector's rude and lascivious conduct disturbs Rahel. Like her mother, she feels vulnerable and ashamed. One of the twins received love and devotion from someone who is now dead. Ammu passes away. Without affection, shelter, and safety, Rahel and Estha are completely disillusioned. Even the church refuses to bury Ammu because she defied the expectations of a caste-based, patriarchal society.Ammu had made an excellent observation "Thanks to our wonderful male-chauvinistic society" (Roy, 57). Ayemenem's harsh and insensitive surroundings scarred both her youth and that of her children. The twins are referred to as baby kochamma "fatherless waifs. Worse still, they were Half-Hindu Hybrids whom no self-respecting Syrian Christian would ever marry" (Roy, 45). She enjoys humiliating them in a horrible manner. She can't stand it when they're comfortable in one other's presence. She emotionally blackmails the twins, shattering their mental state. At the age of eight, she also plays a role in the separation of the twins. Chacko also chastises them for being there when they have no right to be. They are chastised by even the household servant."Tell your mother to take you to your father's house. There you can break as many beds as you like. These aren't your beds. This isn't your house."(Roy, 83)The two egg twins are infatuated with one other and are completely devoted to each other. Estha, who is just seven years old, feels like an outcast in Ayemenem House.

In the work, Arundhati Roy exposes a kid's view of the adult world, as she herself once an unprotected youngster. Her technological ingenuity gives the story a certain appeal. Estha's psychological agony is well described by her. Then there's the most heinous act of child abuse, which causes devastation for the unfortunate kid. After her encounter with the Orangedrink Lemondrink Man at Abhilash Talkies, Estha is absolutely perplexed. The traumatic event continues to haunt the youngster like a nightmare. He doesn't feel safe "the Orangedrink Lemondrink Man could walk in any minute. Catch a Cochin-kottayam bus and be there" (Roy, 194). The ugliness of humanity leaves an indelible mark on his thoughts. He is nevertheless concerned that "the Orangedrink Lemondrink Man could just walk in through the gauze door"(Roy, 197)of the pickle manufacturing plant. His encounters with life's hard realities damage Estha's delicate and naive outlook on life. He is haunted by these two ideas as a result of his traumatic experiences: "(a) Anything can happen to anyone, And (b) It's best to be prepared".(Roy, 194)If that happens, he completely prepares himself to face the worst. Later on, we discover that all of his fears are realised. He begins to lose his feeling of belonging. He solely has feelings for his mother and sister. His mother's tough comments, on the other hand, harm his fragile psyche and push him to adopt drastic measures. She coerces: "I should have dumped you in an orphanage the day you were born. You're the mile stones round my neck just go away why can't you just go away and leave me alone" (Roy, 253). Estha flees her home as a result of this. Estha and Rahel finally settle inside the historical home, an ancient abandoned structure.The twins are requesting an apology from their mother. "What if Ammufinds us and begs us to come back" (Roy, 292) Rahel enquires. "Then we will. But only if she begs", Estha responds (Roy, 292). His perplexity is further expressed in his scratching out his surname from his practise book. "on the front page of book Estha had rubbed out his surname with spit, and taken half the paper with it. Over the whole mass he had written in pencil, Unknown. Esthappen Unknown" (Roy, 156). This episode represents his inner self-erasing rage, which results in self-effacement and disintegration. Rahel, his voice, is no longer with him. For the past 23 years, the inseparable twins have been separated. Estha loses her ability to communicate. Roy discusses the topic of child rearing, which sheds light on the novelist's early years. Ms. Roy has the audacity to depict events in a genuine manner. She speaks openly on subjects that are socially and culturally taboo in the rural areas of South India.The society is built up in such a way that it has little or nothing to offer to unhappy deserted ladies like Ammu, who are literary forsaken everywhere they go, and the worst part is that they are afflicted by those who are referred to as your 'own people.' Arundhati Roy depicts Ammu's life from her childhood through her adolescence to her death. Ammu is shown facing a problematic childhood and terrible nursery years when she had been subjected to all of her father's cruelties done on her and her mother Mammachi, whom her father tore her new pair of shoes in a fit of Schizophrenia. Because she was a female, she was denied a quality education because her father was a frustrated man who, in addition to abusing his wife and children, tore the curtains, kicked the furniture, and destroyed the table lamp. To him, marriage was not a holy union, but rather a symbol of a man's dominance over women.

In Calcutta, Ammu's life takes a new turn when she attends a wedding ceremony. She met her husband there, who was on leave from his job as an Assistant Manager of an Assam tea farm. Ammu made the decision to marry him as soon as possible since she knew her family in Ayemenem would oppose her marriage. As a result, she made a hasty choice to marry him and wrote to her parents, who did not respond. She preferred doing something versus doing nothing. Further evidence of gender prejudice, discrimination, and exploitation can be shown when Ammu is seen being pressured by her husband to please his employer Mr.sexual Hollich's need in order to keep his job. Ammu could no longer bear the humiliation and, after a squabble with her husband, she beat him with a heavy book and fled with her twins (Rahel and Estha) to Ayemenem, where she discovered to her horror that she and her children had been murdered. She sobbed as she watched her two helpless children huddled together in a pitiful state. Ammu's life is damaged as a result of her difficult upbringing and her parents' carelessness, and the same tragedy befalls her own twins. Estha and Rahel, who become sorrowful figures because they have yearned for love, affection, care, and attention their entire lives. In her work *The God of Small Things*, Arundhati Roy wryly reflects on man's double standards, where on the one hand they pretend to love her and uphold her, but on the other hand they desire to control and exploit her relentlessly. They treat her as if she were a toy. Arundhati Roy sought to describe the exploitation of women by a male-dominated society in this way. *The God of Small Things* is a powerful portrayal of women's quest for a legitimate role in society, which is purposely denied to them by patriarchal rules. There's no denying that the social structure of an average Indian woman is fraught with ifs and buts, and this feature of the novel's female characters, such as Ammu, Mammachi, Baby Kochamma, and Margarate Kochamma, has been authentically depicted. Michael Kenny assertsabout The God of Small Things, "Both the novel and its author were celebrated - in the English speaking world and more widely in translation - as the novel was sold in eighteen different countries, within weeks of being published" (Kenny, 1).


*The God of Small Things* explores the atrocities of gender discrimination in India, as well as how patriarchy oppresses and marginalises women in general. The novel's capacity to deal with so many layers of views concerning each member of the Kochamma family's particular family history, as well as more general issues about Kerala in India, is remarkable. She portrays both the plight of untouchables and the reluctance of women seeking fulfillment in their lives. In this work, Roy tells the tragic story of Ammu, the female protagonist, and emphasises how, since infancy, she has been subjected to gender discrimination and has been treated as an useless part of the family when education is denied to her on the grounds of her gender. It is crucial to note that education is a fundamental right of every human being in India, and it must be provided to both men and women without regard to gender, because education is the only thing that may illuminate a person's viewpoint in this contemporary day. Women who are equally deserving members of society should not be denied this right, but this is not the case in this story, since Ammu's parents believe that more education corrupts a lady. As a result of this orthodoxy, Ammu, Pappachi and Mammachi's only daughter, is wrongfully denied the opportunity to pursue higher education by her parents, who believe that higher education degrades a woman. Ammu's parents were guided by this customary notion when they purposefully denied her a college degree. They, on the other hand, made it possible for their son Chacko to complete his studies at Oxford, despite his unexpectedly weak and mediocre academic results. However, because Chacko is a guy, he has access to higher education, whereas his sister does not have the same opportunity because she is a woman. This type of gender discrimination, according to Arundhati Roy, is a terrible injustice and tyranny. She opposes the terrible practise of parents who uphold the traditional viewpoint of prohibiting their daughters from pursuing higher education, a practise that, unfortunately, still exists in the twenty-first century. Meena Usmani's remarks are particularly pertinent in this setting of the novel: The woman have frequently been ruthlessly exploited in our society and the problem is growing day by day. The case of eve teasing, sexual harassment, abduction, rape and wife battering in public and at the work place etc. have been more regularly reported since the 1960s and early 1970s. The issue of violence against women has become the public problem as the women are discriminated at work, home and are denied their due in every field. The constitution of India promises freedom, equality, opportunity and protection to women and give them several rights. Inspite of that they enjoy an unequal status. (Usmani, 13)

Arundhati Roy uses social structures to expose caste differences, gender discrimination, colour and ethnic distinctions, and she strongly believes that these factors impact human connections and individual behavior. The ancient conventions sparked rebellious ideas, and Roy has raised a voice of protest via her characters, strongly portraying the way injustice is done to these socially underprivileged individuals because of their gender. The treatment of women in the character of Ammu for their fundamental needs and passions is abhorrent at a time when fresh waves of change are gathering power, with India's independence and equal rights for women in the constitution. In such a confining environment, Ammu began to feel like a prisoner in the grand Ayemenem House, whereas she yearned to soar high in the sky like a free bird. As a result, she was invited to a wedding function in Calcutta, where she met her future husband, who worked as an Assistant Manager in an Assam tea estate. Ammu intended to marry as quickly as possible, but she soon discovered that her husband was an alcoholic, but the twins Rahel and Estha had already been born. In a male-dominated societal structure, men believe they have the freedom to do anything they want with the opposite sex, which is why Ammu's husband encouraged her to have physical contact with his superior, the tea estate manager, so that he could advance in the firm. Ammu and her children returned to her parents' house as a result of this horrific agony, but she was abused physically and mentally by her parents and brother Chacko without remorse. As a result, Ammu experiences the same fate as Shakespeare's Cordelia in King Lear. She gets penalised because she is a divorced lady who is no longer married to her husband. It's ironic that a divorced daughter is oppressed by her own parents while their estranged son is welcomed and lavished with love and devotion. It is a case of social injustice and discrimination because while Chacko, the estranged son, is treated with kindness by his parents, the same parents are prejudiced towards their daughter because of her helplessness and homelessness. In this regard, it's interesting citing baby Kochamma's envious remark to Ammu that "a married daughter had no standing in her parents' household. "As for a divorced daughter she had no position anywhere at all. As for a divorced daughter from a love marriage, well, words could not describe Baby Kochamma's outrage"(Roy, 45).

Another noteworthy example of gender discrimination and social injustice presented in *The God of Small Things* is women's denial of parental property. Chacko, Ammu's brother, proudly exerts and proclaims his entire right as the inheritor of his parents' property, but Ammu, his sister, is unable to claim any of her parents' property, as a woman has no claim to her father's property. Every now and again, Chacko arrogantly asserts his dominance in front of his sister by saying: "What's yours is mine and what's mine is also mine" (Roy, 57).

This arrogant claim to his land damages his sister's feelings, but Chacko seems unconcerned about hurting her emotionally. The second illustration of Chacko's claim to property is his cooperation with Ammu in running the Paradise Pickle plant. Despite the fact that Ammu works at the factory as much as Chacko, the latter constantly claims it as his own. His constant statement of his entitlement to property suggests that Ammu has been subjected to social injustice. Arundhati Roy sees gender discrimination as not just an act of injustice, but also a kind of societal oppression that she speaks out against.Gender prejudice and patriarchy are thus the key discursive practises that serve as the backdrop to *The God of Small Things* sad story. Ammu was such a character that in her times of sorrow and disaster, her family members who came to see her on the premise of exhibiting sympathy dropped crocodile tears on her misfortunes, and she eventually learned to study their duplicity and loathe them. But it is until Ammu meets Velutha that the true tragedy of her life begins. Despite the fact that Ammu and Velutha belonged to different castes, they both engaged in sex acts out of love and disregard for their respective castes' codes of behaviour. Such an unlawful relationship was not tolerated and was regarded a societal crime that would be harshly punished. Mammachi too had an opinion,"Ammu had defiled the generations of breeding and brought the family to its knees. For generations to come, forever now, people would point at them at sweddings and funerals. At baptism and birthday parties" (Roy, 258).So there is the novel's irony: on the one hand, there is gender discrimination at all levels, while on the other hand, it is astonishing that even women are against women. Both of them are physically separated in the end, with Ammu being imprisoned in her chamber and Velutha being forced to flee the town. The next unfortunate victim of gender discrimination is Ammu's daughter Rahel, who, like her mother, develops a sense of isolation and aloofness in a male-dominated social environment, and is constantly viewed as an outsider by her own family members. Rahel feels like a fish out of water since she is deprived of the Ayemenem House's love, compassion, and care. She goes through the most difficult period of her life after Ammu's death, whether she is at school or at home. Her attitude became cruel and even pathological as a result of the family's treatment.

On the basis of repeated allegations from senior women students, she is even banned and expelled from her convent school.

Rahel attended an architectural school in Delhi and married Larry McCaslin, a research researcher, but her marriage was overshadowed by her divorce. Arundhati Roy's work, according to Wersley, is a genuine picture of the socioeconomic class difficulties that exist in Indian culture. Karl Marx's techniques, on the other hand, are well-suited to the book. The society in this tale has been split according to Marx's idea. Every scene in the novel serves as a soapbox for Roy's views on Indian society. Wealth, occupation, and education have all been shown in a powerful manner, and they have all been associated with an upper-class society in which the lower class has no rights to obtain any of these things. Characters such as Papachi, Mamachi, Baby Kochama, and Chacko have portrayed the higher class, whereas Ammu, Velutha, Rahel, and Estha have shown the poorer class. As a result, the influence on all social issues has been vividly depicted, including physical health, mental health, family life, education, religion, and the criminal justice system. As a result, this study agrees with Roy's assessment that his work depicts societal difficulties of the time and asserts that society has been divided along Marxist and communist lines. He continues by claiming that individuals in any culture have various ideals and qualities. This disparity manifests itself in the form of economic disparities and economic troubles in an individual's social life. He goes on to say that in today's culture, when people are judged on the basis of their social position, the economic problem cannot be ignored or underestimated. Economic discriminations are created in a society that is organised according to Marxist principles, and this discrimination permits money to accrue in the hands of a few people. On this premise, a society with a high level of output has an advantage over a society with a low level of yield.According to Karl Marx, there are three types of social differences that are based on production. He refers to the landowner class as the capitalist or bourgeoisie, the proletariat as the working class, and the labour class as the class that works for the survival of all the other classes. However, the study's goal is to show that Roy's novel *The God of Small Things* raises a slew of class-conscious questions.

Arundhati Roy offers a profound and evocative exploration of gender inequality and the pervasive impact of patriarchy on individual lives and relationships. Through the intricate narratives of her female characters, Roy unveils the multifaceted dimensions of oppression that women endure in a patriarchal society, particularly within the context of the Indian caste system.

Ammu's tragic quest for autonomy and love serves as a poignant illustration of the severe constraints imposed on women who dare to defy societal norms. Her relationship with Velutha, a transgressive act that crosses both caste and gender boundaries, underscores the brutal consequences faced by those who challenge the status quo. Rahel's journey, marked by fragmentation and a search for identity, reflects the long-lasting scars inflicted by a society that punishes women for their desires and choices.

Baby Kochamma's character reveals the complexity of internalized patriarchy, showing how women can become enforcers of the very systems that oppress them. Her actions against Ammu highlight the generational perpetuation of patriarchal values and the profound impact this has on familial and social dynamics.

The intersectionality of caste and gender discrimination is a crucial theme in the novel, illustrating how these axes of oppression compound the suffering of marginalized individuals. The tragic fate of Ammu and Velutha exemplifies the devastating consequences of intersecting social hierarchies, while also emphasizing the radical potential of love as an act of resistance.

Ultimately, *The God of Small Things* calls for a deeper understanding of the systemic forces that perpetuate gender inequality and patriarchy. Roy's narrative compels readers to confront the realities of social injustice and to recognize the resilience and defiance of those who resist oppression. By illuminating the personal and political struggles of her female characters, Roy not only critiques the entrenched systems of discrimination but also advocates for a more equitable and just society.

The exploration of gender inequality and patriarchy in *The God of Small Things* is a testament to the enduring impact of Roy's storytelling. It serves as a powerful reminder of the importance of challenging oppressive structures and amplifying the voices of those who fight for their dignity and agency.

# QUEST FOR IDENTITY

In *The God of Small Things*, Arundhati Roy masterfully intertwines the personal and the political to reveal the deeply ingrained systems of discrimination and oppression that shape the lives of her characters. Among the most poignant and compelling aspects of her narrative is the exploration of gender inequality and the patriarchal structures that confine and define the experiences of women in the story. This chapter delves into the complex portrayals of female characters in the novel, examining their struggles, resistance, and the societal forces that seek to subjugate them.

Ammu, the mother of the twins Estha and Rahel, stands at the center of Roy's critique of gender oppression. Born into a conservative Syrian Christian family, Ammu's life is marked by a series of rejections and restrictions imposed by her gender. Her pursuit of love and independence leads to her defiance of social norms, culminating in a forbidden relationship with Velutha, a man from a lower caste. This act of transgression not only seals her fate but also underscores the severe repercussions that women face for stepping outside the boundaries of patriarchal expectations.

Rahel, Ammu's daughter, embodies the legacy of her mother's struggles. Her fragmented and non-linear narrative reflects the psychological scars inflicted by a society that punishes women for their desires and actions. Rahel's return to Ayemenem after years abroad serves as a journey of reconciliation with her past and an exploration of her own identity, shaped by the same oppressive forces that impacted Ammu.

In stark contrast to Ammu and Rahel, Baby Kochamma represents the internalization and perpetuation of patriarchal norms. Her unfulfilled love and subsequent bitterness manifest in her strict adherence to social hierarchies and her harsh judgment of Ammu's actions. Baby Kochamma's character illustrates how patriarchal values can be upheld by women themselves, often to the detriment of other women.

The novel intricately weaves the issues of caste and gender, highlighting how these axes of discrimination intersect and exacerbate the oppression experienced by women. Ammu's relationship with Velutha is a powerful narrative device that exposes the dual burden of caste and gender oppression. The severe societal backlash they face serves to illustrate the compounded discrimination that arises when these two systems of hierarchy collide.

Roy portrays love as a radical act of resistance against the oppressive structures of caste and gender. Ammu's and Velutha's love, though ultimately tragic, symbolizes a defiance of the rigid social order. Similarly, Rahel's bond with her twin brother Estha is a source of solace and rebellion against the constraints imposed on them. Through these relationships, Roy suggests that love, in its purest form, transcends social boundaries and challenges the status quo.

The quest for agency among the female characters is a central theme that highlights the pervasive nature of patriarchy and the resilience required to confront it. Ammu and Rahel's stories, marked by defiance and suffering, reflect the broader struggle of women to assert their identities and reclaim their narratives in a society that seeks to silence them. By bringing these stories to light, Arundhati Roy not only critiques the patriarchal structures of her time but also calls for a deeper understanding and dismantling of these enduring systems of oppression.

Through this exploration of gender inequality and patriarchy, this chapter aims to provide readers with a nuanced understanding of the challenges faced by the women in *The God of Small Things*, and the ways in which their quests for agency resonate with broader social and political issues.

The story depicts the sorrows of three generations of women—Mammachi, Ammu, and Rahel—each of whom reacts differently to the circumstances. The three generations of women have diverse perspectives on life and respond to situations in various ways. Regardless of the difficulties they faced or the eras in which they lived, the lives of women protagonists in the majority of books showed an eventual struggle. They were not prepared to surrender to the predefined political structures of society or family.

Mammachi is an excellent example of an older generation of women who submissively accept patriarchal culture. She is a "adarshbhartiyanaari" who considers that a woman's primary responsibility is to her husband and that she should at all costs yield to his whims and fancies. Mammachi has spent her entire life as a victim of her husband's abuse. Either her husband beats her with a brass vase or a riding crop with an ivory handle. Mammachi, especially on the violin, has excellent musical skill, but her husband Pappachi is envious of her. When his wife's violin instructor makes the error of informing him that she is exceptionally skilled and possibly concert class, the plot thickens. Later, he smashes the violin's bow and dumps it into the river one night. She began a pickle-making company, which caused Pappachi to feel envious once more. Pappachi declines to assist her since manufacturing pickles is not an appropriate career for high-ranking ex-government officials. As a result, their marriage lacks communication, affection, and cooperation. Mammachi's unquestioning adherence to patriarchy is more of a protective stance than an actual consent to be ruled by them. Chacko, her rich and Oxford-educated son, was the second guy who controlled Mammachi's life. He takes over Mammachi's pickle plant when he returns home following his divorce with Margaret, referring to the factory as "my factory, my pineapples, my pickles" (Roy, 57) without taking into account Mammachi, who established and built the factory before Chacko went back home. Mammachi did nothing except silently take it. Being a moral woman, she tolerated her husband's actions because they were supported by the community.

Ammu is a woman from the second generation. She is the new lady who makes a great effort to resist the patriarchal structure that rules Indian society. Men as well as women double her marginalisation. Because of her gender, she was denied affection and attention as a youngster. Due to the typical patriarchal family system, where a girl's birth is undesirable and is seen as a burden on the family, her father beat her ruthlessly with an iron-topped riding crop. Her brother Chacko, in contrast, enjoys special treatment in every facet of family life just because he is a man. While her brother gets sent to Oxford for higher studies once Ammu finishes school, this is because "Pappachi insisted that a college education was an unnecessary expense for a girl. So Ammu had no choice but to leave Delhi and move with them" (Roy, 38). As a result, her own family stands in the way of her independence and continued advancement. Ammu's existence is consumed by boredom, solitude, and waiting for marriage proposals after her family relocates from Delhi to Ayemenem. She is enthralled with her home in Ayemenem and longs fervently to know who she is: "There was little for young girl to do in Ayemenem other than to wait for marriage proposals while she helped her mother with the housework… All day she dreamed of escaping from Ayemenem and the clutches of her ill tempered father and bitter, long-suffering mother." (Roy, 38-39)

Her father consents to letting her spend the summer in Calcutta with a distant aunt. She meets her future husband there, at a wedding reception, and marries him without hesitation or shame, believing that by doing so, she would be able to stop her painful relationship with her parents. But tragically, her misfortune "her husband turns out to be not just a heavy drunkard but a full-blown alcoholic" (Roy, 40). Ammu, who had recently arrived to Assam with her husband, quickly rose to prominence in the Planters' Club. She carried a silver lame handbag on a chain and wore backless blouses with her saris. She also learnt how to blow flawless smoke rings while smoking long cigarettes in a silver cigarette holder, which helped to remove the patriarchal dominance that was present in Indian society. Ammu, a young lady, refuses to submit to the male-chauvinist social structure's control. Her disastrous marriage, which began when her drunken husband offered her to his English employer for his career possibilities, allowed her to flee the suffocating environment of her parents' house. She does not submit to her new master (husband); rather, she divorces him in order to preserve her individuality and sense of self. She cannot accept her husband's terrible behaviour, unlike her mother, and would rather get a divorce than blindly maintain her marriage, which would go against Indian society's communal norms. She returns to Ayemenem unwanted "to everything she had fled from only a few years ago, except that now she had two young children and no more dreams" (Roy, 42). Ammu had a terrible marriage experience; she suffers physically and mentally because of her spouse. She questions marriage, which, in the words of Michael Foucault, appears to be more of a disciplinary institution that works to control and silence those who stand out, as if they were lunatics who need to be reasoned with or imprisoned. She fights against such social institutions. Ammu's treatment as an outsider in her own family as a result of being the victim of an unhappy marriage determines her status in society. It is extremely odd that, because a divorced woman is deemed non virtuous, a daughter who is alienated from her husband is tortured and persecuted in her parents' home. Contrarily, an estranged son named Chacko is not only warmly welcomed but also continues to be the legitimate heir to the family's riches and fortune. Mammachi encourages him when he flirts with a poor woman under the guise of 'man's needs', (Roy, 268) While Ammu's romance with paravanVelutha is viewed as illegal, unconventional, and wicked. Despite everything, the new lady in Ammu decides to love the guy her children adored during the day while breaking the four walls of the house that had previously encased her. Ammu's obsession with Velutha crosses caste, social, and religious borders and builds something of a revolt against her being treated differently because she is a woman by breaking the love laws that her community has enforced. Ammu's defiance of parental and marital conventions, as well as her relationship with the dark-skinned, untouchable Velutha, represent violations of a fixed social order that supports the unalterable rules of love. Even though Ammu is well aware of the traditional nature of her community, she nevertheless takes the risk of dating

Velutha. This demonstrates Ammu's frantic need for love, which neither her parents nor her husband were able to fulfil. The children's greatest friend is Velutha since they feel alone in Ayemenm due of their mother's divorce. The little time the kids had Velutha's companionship allowed them to experience genuine joy. Unfortunately, Velutha's father informs Mammachi about Ammu and Velutha's covert relationship. Due to Mammachi's inability to tolerate Ammu's cross-caste relationship, Velutha is taken by the police and slain on the pretext of rape. Ammu is severely humiliated when she goes to the police station to correct the situation: "Kottayam police does not take statement from Veshyas (prostitutes) and their illegitimate children" (Roy, 58).

As a result, Ammu receives harsh treatment from the police, which is said to turn lawbreakers around. She is also confined by Kerala's Syrian Christian community's traditional family structure and inheritance rules. Ammu's family ultimately banishes her from her house. She is not permitted to visit Ayemenem and is separated from her children. She strives frantically to look for a nice job in secret locations. This demonstrates her attempt to find her actual identity but failure. She is discovered dead in a filthy room at the Bharat Lodge in Aleppy after being worn out, unwell, and ultimately defeated. Even when she passes away, the church refuses to bury Ammu, so her humiliation continues. Finally, she is incinerated in an electric crematorium where only abandoned people and people who died while in police custody are burned. Before Ammu accepts this fate, she makes hasty attempts at self-realization and transforms into a symbol of all subalterns, particularly women, who oppose the social order's power structures.

Rahel is a third generation family member. Comparatively speaking to Ammu and Mammachi, she is a less minor figure. She doesn't experience domestic abuse as others do, but because she is the daughter of the mistreated Ammu, she is still on the outside looking in. Like her mother, she was subjected to ridicule and humiliation as a youngster. Because of the distressing recollections of the past, her life is completely disrupted and abandoned. When Rahel challenges the grownups, they threaten to expel her and inform her that it is inappropriate "people love her a little less" (Roy, 112). Rahel's self-perception as someone who may not be likeable is influenced by this reprimand. Ammu is terrified by her children's behaviour since she has learned not to love or trust anybody because dread might appear to be something it is not "willingness to love people who didn't really love them and (it) sometimes made her want to hurt them-just as an education, a protection" (Roy, 43). Rahel develops uneasiness and worry as a result of Ammu's mistrust of other people, which teaches Rahel that love is not something to take for granted, but rather something constrained and conditional. Rahel's character is continually plagued by the dread of not being loved, and her readiness to suffer penalties might be interpreted as a continuation of this. "Ammu",

Rahel said, 'shall I miss dinner as my punishment?' she was keen to exchange punishments. No dinner, in exchange for Ammu loving her the same as before" (Roy, 11). Rahel is disturbed and refuses to eat when Ammu doesn't reprimand her "hoping that if she could somehow effect her own punishment, Ammu would rescind hers" (Roy, 115). This demonstrates Rahel's passionate search for love.

Rahel is a lady who does not fit in with her family or the wider community. She observes the egregious injustices meted out to her mother as she resides in her grandparents' home. She becomes a liberated lady who, unlike her mother, is not constrained by the restrictions of conventional norms as she grows up unloved. Due to her preoccupation with her twin brother Estha, Rahel was also unable to enjoy a happy married life. The story therefore portrays the dried-out souls of women from a certain socioeconomic setting. The work also shows attempts to defy patriarchal conventions. By reading the posters backwards, Rahel and Estha are defying patriarchal norms. Readers are persuaded to read the book backwards by the novel itself. In a number of instances, the characters dare to step outside of their comfort zones. Ammu breaks the rules of womanly virtues and dares to forget that she is a touchable who shouldn't let an untouchable approach her. Velutha dares to forget his untouchability. Forgetting about "Locusts Stand I," Ammu dares to feel at home in Ayemenem. The breakdown of patriarchal standards results in catastrophe. The rules are only known by Chacko: "What is mine is mine. What is yours is also mine"(Roy, 28). In essence, this is the patriarchal code that must be followed. The heroes of Roy's story dared to disobey this commandment, but not without suffering severe consequences. The History House imposes laws and punishes any transgressions that occur in the Ayemenem House.

Roy might be seen as the definition of her feminine style. Ammu pushes the limits of who and how much is acceptable; she rejects all phallocentric rhetoric in order to herald a new era in which women will make their own decisions, even if those choices include dying alone in a desolate location.As a result, when she returns to Ayemenem, she responds to an old man who inquires about her marital status by saying, "We're divorced" (Roy, 130) without being concerned about what the elderly guy may think of her response. Rahel evolved as a strong individual despite her trials and sufferings.

# 5

*The God of Small Things* is told in a succession of flashbacks and recollections that take place between 1969 and 1993. The reader is permitted to piece together his own image by linking fragments of memory. In 1997, it was awarded the Man Booker Prize. Women are treated more or less severely in all generations through this story.As a result, Roy sends the message that everyone should be treated equally, and that no caste structure or gender identity in society should be based on justice and chances. The author depicts the unwelcome pains of women who must endure interminable torment in silence in his work *The God Of Small Things*. Women must speak out against a patriarchal culture dominated by males. Arundhati Roy addresses gender bias in her novel *The God of Small Things* in a compelling and accessible way. The story shows the unpleasant sufferings that women must bear in quiet and humility.In her work *The God of Small Things*, Roy depicts the wretched fate of women in a male-dominated social environment and fiercely supports the feminine cause. It is the novelist's heroic endeavour to elicit social consciousness among females and subalterns, and Roy has defined the sad fate of women in a male-dominated societal set-up and passionately supports the female cause via the conflict between the powerful and the helpless. Not only that, but the novel had her seated in the first row. She gained fame among the readers after that. This is a one-of-a-kind work in which the author boldly combines all storytelling approaches, resulting in the development of a new style – a new invention. As a result, Ammu, who wants to be in charge of her life, is confronted with a system in which Chacko, her "Marxist" brother, abuses the impoverished women workers at his business, both financially and sexually, and goes unchecked. Ammu sees patriarchy usurp and suffocate personalities like Mammachi.Velutha is accused of the fortunate drowning of Sophie Mol and Pappachi, Ammu's father, is doubtful of her Bengali Hindu husband's desire to prostitute her in order to satisfy his white boss. Ammu, a subaltern who is both economically and socially oppressed, challenges the colonial masters' authority. Ammu, suffocated by social injustice, rebels against the Syrian Christian community in Kerala's social conventions. This uprising is a kind of defiance against the society's core underpinnings. Her most important behaviour, becoming sexually involved with the 'Untouchable,' lower-class Velutha, cannot be seen just as a sexual violation. In summary, Ammu fights the oppressive and exploitative political and social systems as a woman and as a subaltern.Despite her failure to make any significant changes, she fights valiantly to realise her aspirations. Ammu's peculiarity stems from the fact that, while she may not have worked specifically for other subalterns, all of her efforts were aimed towards liberating other types of subalterns.Arundhati Roy's work *The God of Small Things* is a manuscript that vividly illustrates the conflict between classes. Not only has the novel highlighted the class conflict, but it also asserts that the top classes constantly exploit the lower classes for their own gain. It has been attempted to represent the lowest level of society being exploited by the upper classes through the characters. Velutha, the novel's protagonist, is the voice of society's lowest classes, and he is revealed to be a person who is below the level of humanity. He has no right to touch anyone, even humans, because he belongs to the untouchable class. Roy aims to demonstrate that the top class of society has established some rules, which they then use for personal gain. On the other hand, it is also stated that the social problems that exist in India are so enormous that people in India appear to be members of a superstitious culture who believe that if they touch something untouchable, something bad would happen to them. Similarly, it is considered a transgression if a person from the lower social class seeks to have love relationships with someone from the upper social class. The entire society will then be against him. Because Velutha is untouchable, he has no right to love any touchable woman.

As a result, Roy's characters are strong, courageous women. They illustrate the fluidity of tradition, questioning its status as a closed phenomena. On the one hand, the story explores a cross-caste love connection and its ramifications, while on the other, it addresses problems such as the daughter's entitlement to inherit her parents' land. The three generations of women described in the story each have their own perspectives on life and approach it in various ways. The novel's disparate treatment of males and females causes social imbalance, resulting in much of the misery and discontent found in families, as well as the deterioration of children's lives. As a result, we have a paralysed society that is incapable and unwilling to evolve. On the other hand, it is also stated that the social problems that exist in India are so enormous that people in India appear to be members of a superstitious culture who believe that if they touch something untouchable, something bad would happen to them. Similarly, it is considered a transgression if a person from the lower social class seeks to have love relationships with someone from the upper social class. Then the entire society will turn against him. Because Velutha is untouchable, he has no right to fall in love with a touchable woman. Because he works at a factory, he is also a communist party member. Because he is slain by a lady who belongs to a high social taboo, his death is political. The bourgeoisie has complete freedom, while the proletariat lacks even the most basic necessities of existence. Similarly, the work addresses the question of how Indian society should be. Roy, as a socialist, is concerned about the state of society, in which social conventions are so annoying that human beings are no longer placed on the pedestal of human beings.

*Echoes of Marginalization: Unveiling Social Discrimination in Arundhati Roy's The God of Small Things* encapsulates the profound exploration of social discrimination within the novel. Arundhati Roy's masterpiece, *The God of Small Things,* meticulously examines the intricate layers of marginalization, revealing how deeply ingrained social hierarchies perpetuate injustice and inequality.

Through the lens of the novel, we witness the devastating impact of caste discrimination on individuals such as Velutha, Ammu, and Baby Kochamma. Roy's narrative exposes the structural violence inherent in society, where marginalization is not merely a personal experience but a systemic oppression rooted in historical and cultural frameworks.

The characters in the novel embody the struggle against societal norms that dictate who holds power and who is subjugated. Roy's portrayal of Velutha, a talented carpenter who faces brutal persecution for daring to love across caste boundaries, exemplifies the tragic consequences of defying entrenched social hierarchies.

Moreover, the narrative style of "The God of Small Things" itself disrupts conventional storytelling, reflecting the disjointed reality faced by marginalized individuals whose lives are fragmented by prejudice and discrimination. Roy's prose serves as a powerful tool to confront and challenge the reader's perception of social norms and injustices.

This book underscores the enduring relevance of Roy's novel in shedding light on the pervasive nature of social discrimination. It invites readers to critically examine how inequality manifests and persists in society, urging us to confront our complicity in systems that perpetuate marginalization.

This novel serves not only as a literary triumph but also as a poignant critique of the deep-seated social discrimination that continues to shape and constrain lives. It compels us to reflect on our roles in dismantling these barriers and striving towards a more just and equitable world.

In this novel the theme of gender inequality resonates profoundly, revealing the pervasive and insidious nature of social discrimination. Through the lives of characters like Ammu and Velutha, Roy illuminates how deeply entrenched societal norms perpetuate unequal treatment based on gender. Women like Ammu face marginalization on multiple fronts: economically, socially, and politically. Their identities are shaped and constrained by rigid patriarchal structures that deny them agency and self-determination.

The novel portrays how gender roles dictate behavior and opportunities, relegating women to subordinate positions both within the family and in society at large. Ammu's struggle for autonomy and love is emblematic of countless women whose aspirations are stifled by a culture that prioritizes male dominance and control. Roy critiques this system through poignant narratives that expose the personal and emotional costs of gender discrimination.

Moreover, Roy's exploration of identity extends beyond gender to encompass broader themes of caste and class. Velutha's tragic fate underscores how intersecting forms of marginalization exacerbate social inequalities, denying individuals like him the right to a dignified existence simply because of their social status.

It serves as a powerful indictment of a society where marginalized identities are systematically oppressed and denied full humanity. Roy challenges readers to confront these injustices and imagine a world where identity is not a basis for discrimination but a source of pride and empowerment. Through her lyrical prose and nuanced characterizations, Roy compels us to reconsider our own roles in perpetuating or challenging systems of inequality, urging us towards a future where all individuals can live free from the echoes of marginalization.

Through the lives of Ammu, Velutha, and others, Roy unveils the harsh realities faced by those deemed 'untouchable' in Indian society. The narrative exposes how untouchability perpetuates a system of marginalization, denying individuals their basic humanity and dignity.

Throughout the novel, Roy paints a poignant picture of the consequences of untouchability on individuals and communities. Velutha, despite his intelligence and skills, is relegated to the margins of society solely because of his caste. His forbidden love with Ammu underscores the deeply ingrained prejudices that dictate social interactions and relationships. Their tragic fate highlights the impossibility of transcending caste barriers in a society steeped in discrimination.

Moreover, Ammu's experiences further illustrate the intersectionality of caste with gender, class, and personal agency.

As a woman from a socially privileged background who falls in love with an 'untouchable' man, she faces double the stigma and consequences. Her defiance of societal norms ultimately leads to her own marginalization and tragic separation from her children.

Roy's portrayal of untouchability serves as a powerful critique of India's caste system and its enduring legacy of social inequality. By confronting readers with the harsh realities faced by marginalized communities, she challenges us to acknowledge and dismantle the structures of oppression that continue to define and limit lives. Through *The God of Small Things*, Roy compels us to confront the echoes of marginalization, urging us towards a more just and inclusive society where every individual can be seen, valued, and respected regardless of caste, class, or gender.

# Bibliography


Agarwal, Bala, Anju,*Post-Independence Indian Writing in English*, Author Press, New Delhi, 2008.

Alam, Khurshid. *Untouchables in The God of Small Things*, Postcolonial web, 17, Jan. 2005.

Ahmad, Aijaz, *Reading Arundhati Roy politically*, In Murari Prasad,Arundhati Roy: Critical Perspectives, New Delhi, India: Pencraft International, 2006.

Bhatta, Indira, *Arundhati Roy's The God of small Things*, Creative Books, New Delhi, 1919.

Beavior, Simone de. *The Second Sex, London*, Vintage series, 2011.

Chandra, Tirthankar, *Sexual/Textual Strategies in The God of Small Things*, Commonwealth Essays and Studies, 1997.

Darlymple, William, Harpers and Queen, *Praise for the God of Small Things*, TGST, New Delhi: Penguin Books, 2002.

Dirks, N,*Castes of Mind: Colonialism and the Making of Modern India*. Mumbai: Goharpubulshirs.

Flynn, Travis, *Arundhati Roy*, University of Minnesota, 1, Jan. 2006.

Ganaie, Altaf Ahmad, *Social Realism in Arundhati Roy's Novel "The God of Small Things"*, Indian Journal of Applied Research, 2014.Ganguly, Debjani, Caste, *Colonialism and Counter Modernity*, Routledge, 2005.

Ghosh, Pragati,*Short Summary of "The God of Small Things"* by Arundhati Roy.

Ismail. K. Mohammed,*Cultural Narratives in Arundhati Roy's the God of Small Things*: *A Critical Analysis.*

International Journal of English Language, Literature and Humanities, 2014.

Kamble, S.D. & G.V.Jadhav, *Marginalization of Women in Arundhati Roy's The God of Small Things*, Research Front 2013.

K.B Sunderan, *The God of small Things: A saga of Lost Dreams*, Atlandic publication, New Delhi, 2000.

Kenny, Michael, *Novelist Arundhati Roy Finds Fame Abroad, Infamy at Home*,The Boston Globe 5 August 1997.

K.M. Pandey, *The Small God Made Big:Arundhati Roy's The God Of Small Things,* from Arundhati Roy's Fictional World, A N Dwivedi, B R, publishing 2008.

Kunhambu K, *Search for Identity in Arundhathi Roy's Novel*, International Journal of Scientific & Technology Research,2014.

Pandian, I.D. Arundhati Roy: Life and Work, Bhaskar Publication, 2009.

Prasad, Amar Nath,Arundhati Roy's *The God of Small Things: A Critical Appraisal*, New Delhi: Sarup& Sons, 2004.

Prasad, Murari, Introduction, In Murari Prasad,*Arundhati Roy: Critical perspectives*, New Delhi, India, Pencraft International, 2006.

Rajimwale, Sharad. Arundhati Roy's *The God of Small Things: A Critical Appraisal*, New Delhi: Rama Brothers India Pvt. Ltd., 2006.

Roy, Arundhati. *The God of Small Things* New Delhi: Penguin Books India Pvt.limiteds, 2002

Roy, Arundhati, *The God Of Small Things*. Great Britain: Flamingo,1997.

Roy, Arundhati. *The God of Small Things*, New Delhi, IndiaInk, 1997. Print.

Roy, Arundhati, *The God of Small Things*, Penguin, India 2002.

Roy, Amitabh. *The God of small things: A Novel of Social Commitment*, New Delhi: Atlantic Publishers and Distributors, 2005.

R.S Sharma, Arundhati Roy's *The God of small Things* (ed.), Atlantic pub. New Delhi, 1919.

Sahu, Nandini,*The Post-Colonial Space: Writing the Self and the Nation*, Atlantic, 2007.

Sarode, D. A. S. *Victims of Social Discrimination in 'The God of Small Things'*. Smart Moves Journal Ijellh, 2015.

Sonia, *Social Consciousness in Arundhati Roy's The God of Small Things*, Language in India, 2013.

Usmani, Meena, "*Violence against Women*" University News Magazine, 2000.

# About the Author

Dr. Prabha Parmar is a dedicated and insightful literary scholar with a passion for examining the complex social issues embedded in contemporary literature. She earned her M.A. and Ph.D. in English from C.C.S. University, Meerut, where she developed a deep understanding of how literature reflects and critiques societal structures. Her academic work focuses on uncovering the hidden layers of meaning within literary texts, particularly the interplay between narrative technique and social commentary. Her areas of specialization include Indian English Literature, American Literature, and Translation Studies.

With over 15 publications in national and international journals, Dr. Parmar has made significant contributions to her field. She has presented numerous research papers at various seminars and conferences and brings more than twelve years of teaching experience to her current role. Her past positions include lecturer roles at J.V. Jain College, Saharanpur, and the Punjab Institute of Engineering & Applied Research, as well as Assistant Professor at R.O.G. Degree College, Bhagwanpur, Shri Guru Ram Rai University, Dehradun, and Haridwar University, Roorkee. Currently, she serves as an Associate Professor at the Faculty of Arts, Humanities and Social Sciences at Motherhood University, Roorkee Uttarakhand.

# About the Co-author

Shahjadi Ansari was born and raised in Mohammadpur Kunhari Sultanpur, a small village in the Haridwar district of Uttarakhand. Currently, she is pursuing her Doctorate in English Literature from Shri Guru Ram Rai University Dehradun Uttarakhand. She completed her Bachelor's degree at Hemvati Nandan Bahuguna Garhwal University in Uttarakhand and earned her Master's degree in English from the same, graduating as a Gold Medalist. During the 7th convocation of HNB Garhwal University, she was awarded a Gold Medal for her academic excellence.

A dedicated scholar, Shahjadi has presented numerous research papers at seminars and conferences across the country, many of which have been published in prestigious national and international journals. At a national seminar organized by the Welfare Forum for Universal Research Scholars and Professors, she was honored with the Best Research Paper Award. In 2022, she published her first book titled *Introduction to English Prose: A Study Guide BA I Semester English Literature*, ISBN- 9798891862661.

Currently, Shahjadi is engaged in studying the impact of the 1947 Partition on literature and society. With over four years of teaching experience, she is currently a lecturer in the Department of English at Garg PG College in Laksar, Haridwar, Uttarakhand. She has also held lecturer positions at Nimbus Academy of Management and Baba Farid Institute of Technology, both located in Dehradun.